from Wailing *to* Worship

*My Journey to Joy
In the Midst of Loss*

Tarus R. Porter

FROM WAILING TO WORSHIP
My Journey to Joy In the Midst of Loss

Tarus Porter
tarus4243@yahoo.com

ISBN: 978-1-949826-51-7

Published by: EAGLES GLOBAL BOOKS | Frisco, Texas
In conjunction with the 2022 Eagles Authors Course
Cover & interior designed by DestinedToPublish.com

Foreword

My sisters and dear friends of every age and cultural background, please understand that grief, loss, and depression have no boundaries. They have and will affect us all at different stages of development. They do not automatically infect the rhythm of our breathing and living life. God desires us to cast our cares upon HIM and be ever so careful to honor and worship HIM all our days.

From Wailing to Worship speaks to these authentic experiences in the life of my sister Tarus Porter. Journey with her as she wailed, prayed, believed, praised, and wsorshipped through it all. The pure intensity of death, grief, loss, and hurt caused her to wail. But oh, how our God nurtured and restored her gently to worship from an elevated place. It is in that lofty place that He blessed her to be such a beautiful vessel of honor before HIM!

Dr. Kina Nicole Arnold
Yahweh Beaute Inc and PURe Beaute Inc
<small>HIS BRIDE INTIMATE CONVERSATIONS</small>
www.kinArnold.com

Dedication

This book is dedicated to those who have found themselves in the valley of darkness due to the traumatic loss of a loved one. May the God of light shine brightly on you as you find the courage and obedience to worship your way to the mountaintop of Joy, Peace, Tranquility, and Wholeness.

"Arise, shine, for your light has come, and the glory of the Lord rises upon you." Isaiah 60:1 New International Version

Acknowledgments

To my Abba Father, Elohim, and El Roi: You knew before I did what I would and would not be able to endure. You have loved, comforted, shielded, and forgiven me even when I did not deserve it. THANK YOU for your Grace, Mercy, and Patience. You waited for me and for THIS, I shall ALWAYS Worship and Dedicate My Life to Serving You.

My Angels—Mommy, Daddy, and Teia: No words can express how much I miss you, and not a day goes by that I don't think about each of you. Thank you for being the best parents that you knew how to be. I was truly Blessed to be your daughter. Because of you both, I am the strong woman that stands today. Teia, although you were a bug, you grew into one of the most admirable people I know. Your strength through your illness and how you were still full of life made me proud to be your big sister. I will forever love you all always.

My King on Earth—LeAnton Porter: When God reunited us, He knew it was our time to be together. You are my best friend, confidant, prayer warrior, covering, priest, and lover of my soul. Thank you for your never-ending support, encouragement, motivation, and unconditional love for me, flaws and all. I am loved because You love Me, which makes Me love You even more.

My Miracle—Jason L. Bender: You are God's Gift to Me. That is the literal meaning of your name, in addition to Healer. Your birth brought a change to my life for the better and until I saw your face, I never knew how much a tiny human being could make me fall in love over and over again every day. I am proud to say that my hard work as a mommy has paid off, as you have grown to be a loving, kind, intelligent, and respectful young man. You are my Sonshine, the Joy of my heart, and no matter how old you get, you will always be my baby.

Sisters—Talisa, TaShawna, and Ladia: You three have been my rocks since our parents passed and I don't know how I would have made it without you. The little sisters stepped up to take care of their big sister and the strength you provided helped me to stand. Thank you for loving and taking care of me when I needed you most and when I should have been taking care of you. That means Number 1 did a good job as a big sister and I taught you all well—ha! Together we stand united, as we are each other's keepers, and nothing shall ever break our bond.

Momtie—Dorothy Woods: From the womb until now you have been the one that I've run to, confided in, cried to, and received

Godly advice from. You consider me the daughter you never had, and you have always shown me unconditional love. You've never been judgmental; you have always been honest, and you have taught me about forgiveness. Thank you for allowing me to glean from you and for instilling in me my first moments of prayer, praise, and worship. I love you beyond what words can express.

Dr., Min. Kina Arnold: *From mentor, to teacher, to big sister, you have been there for me through some of my most traumatic moments in life and no amount of deeds or words can express my love and how grateful I am for you. Your sincere love, care, concern, time, patience, and sowing into me are what make me admire and love you. Thank you for your trust, encouragement, correction, and motivation, and for being the Amazing Big Sister that I've always wanted.*

Pastor Orlando Dallas: *My Pastor and friend. Thank you for showing me how to worship. From the pulpit to the streets, you were evidence of what worship looked like. I thank you for supporting and pushing me to believe in myself and my gift of movement. Your heart and love for people were to be commended. From the pulpit until your last breath, you were a worshipper, and I'm grateful that I was able to be under your covering to see it all. I Miss You, Man of God.*

Min. Tammy Chambers: *Thank you for being obedient to my ask, which turned into God's divine plan for you. It is because of you that I learned to "Worship as if my life depends on it" and that "I am a Masterpiece because I am a Piece of the Master." Your* *gifting to the Kingdom is to be admired and not taken lightly. You have become one of my closest friends and my covenant sister whom I love dearly.*

Generals in the Kingdom—Dr. Pamela Hardy (EITI/TEN), Min. Michelle Davis, and Pastor Valencia Lacy (Altar Church of Worship): *You ALL have played a major role in my growth in the ministry of movement. You have guided me all the way, from giving me my first glimpse of it, to teaching me about it, to sending me to answer the call, to allowing me to minister under your leadership, and for this I say, "I am grateful." Your love, kindness, pouring, training, correction, and equipping so I could go forth in humility and excellence as a Kingdom Ambassador have not been in vain. My prayer is that as I continue to grow, the Dunamis power that you all have will fall on me like a wind of fire as we all continue to Glorify Jesus and Lift His Name High.*

My Beloved Leader—Monica Beverly (Passa): *Thank you for being a bright light on earth as you are now in heaven. I honor you as my leader, friend and covenant sister, and it was my pleasure to serve you. It has been tough to do ministry without seeing your beautiful face and hearing your boisterous laugh. I can no longer listen to "We Lift You Up" by Miranda Curtis or "Grace" by Dante Bowe without thinking about you. You did what you were created to do and that was to leave a positive mark on this earth. You were loved because of the love you gave and you are deeply missed. Thank you to the Beverly and Gardner Family for sharing your Beloved Monica with us.*

Epigraph

Go, find Your place of worship
Look into Your pain and find Your praise
Every low place in Your life
Prepared You for your high place

Every tear You cried
Was water for the garden of Your victory
And even though You're in the valley
Victory comes through Your adversity
Go, find Your place of worship

Written By: Jason Nelson (Songwriter/Singer)

Table of Contents

Introduction

"Yet the Lord longs to be gracious to you; therefore he will rise up to show you compassion. For the Lord is a God of justice. Blessed are all who wait for him!"
Isaiah 30:18 (New International Version)

"Enough is Enough! How much pain can one person take?" Dealing with loss over and over again can become exhausting and draining. Especially when it is personal. One can only endure so much trauma before becoming broken. This was the consistent conversation that I would have with myself over and over again, but what I learned is that either I am going to allow every horrible, tragic, life altering thing in my life to drive me insane (which it almost did), or I am going to learn how to Press and Worship my way through it all. Not allowing your flesh to manifest is easier said than done, but I made the decision to choose the latter and was amazed at how, in those times when I got so deeply depressed, withdrawn, and angry that (to be transparent) I didn't want to be in God's presence, I knew that the only way I was going to survive mentally, emotionally, spiritually, and physically was to fight my way back, even if most of the time that meant me kicking, screaming, crying, and/or crawling. I am still alive today because God loved me more than I loved myself and more than anyone else could have. He waited for me, for which I am truly grateful!

My realization going through this journey is that my brokenness led me to a lifestyle of worship. As hard as it was, my sacrifice and obedience in worshipping God in the midst of my grief and pain made me grow stronger in Him, and I was reminded of His faithfulness. My surrender led to my breakthrough and my breakthrough led to my freedom.

Upon reading this book, I pray that you, the reader, realize that you are not alone, regardless of what you think or how you feel, but that with Jesus Christ, you can attain joy, peace and tranquility again if you worship Him. I pray that my transparency and sharing of some of my most intimate "life's happenings" will encourage, uplift, and comfort you, and enable you to allow God to deliver and heal you into wholeness as you receive revelation and acquire a closer relationship with Him; one that leads to freedom, self-love, and a desire to worship with *Abba* Father more.

My journey was predestined before I was created, and only God knew what I would be able to endure even when I felt that I could not. Jesus was my help, but only when I allowed myself to cry out and let Him. That's the key. Desperation has a sound, and you have to become the Altar in order for God's will to be done. As you seek God and stay in His presence, may your life become fulfilled and may your wailing turn into worship….just as mine did!

> *"Those who cleanse themselves from the latter will be instruments for special purposes, made holy, useful to the master and prepared to do a good work."*
> **2 Timothy 2:21**

Chapter 1

Wailing…Born into It

Miriam Webster's Dictionary defines *wailing* as: (v.) to express sorrow audibly: lament: to make a sound suggestive of a mournful cry: to express dissatisfaction: complain

> (n.) a usually prolonged cry or sound expressing grief or pain: a sound suggestive of wailing: a querulous expression of grievance: complaint: the practice of wailing: loud lamentation.

The King James Bible defines *wailing* as: (v.) to lament; to moan; to bewail; to weep; to express sound audibly

> (n.) loud weeping; violent lamentation.

Types of wailing include sobbing, weeping, bawling, bewailing, blubbering, howling.

"Lord, you are my God; I will exalt you and praise your name, for in perfect faithfulness you have done wonderful things, things planned long ago."
Isaiah 25:1

When a child is born, the first thing they do is let out a loud wail. This lets everyone know that the child is healthy. Some say that the louder the wail, the stronger the child will be. You never know, when you are born, that God is purposely preparing you for something greater in your life when he puts you through certain tests and trials, especially when it pertains to dealing with the loss of life, whether of family or friends. Everyone either has or will experience this in some form or fashion, but for me it occurred a few months after I was born; it was the death of my paternal grandmother, my father's mother, who was unfortunately murdered. Was I able to emotionally experience this loss at that time? Of course not, but after learning the details of her death when I got older, I felt a sense of sorrow, grief, sadness, and anger, because I was robbed of being able to establish a relationship with a woman who I was told would have loved me tremendously, especially since I was her first granddaughter.

Out of four siblings, I am the oldest born to my parents. I say that God has a knee-slapping sense of humor sometimes, because we were born eight, sixteen, and eighteen years apart and all girls. When I tell people this, their first response is usually "Wow!" Some of my experiences into and throughout my adulthood have been great, some good, some bad, some outright horrible; some I could control, some I couldn't, and some I purposely blocked out of my memory but they somehow crept their way back into my thoughts. I often tell people, "My short-term memory sucks, but my long-term memory is amazing," and it really is; I can remember specific details of things from the time I was three years old. Some of those memories initially caused me some anxiety when I got older because they had me reflecting on my life's journey.

The revelation I came to was that I have in fact had more trauma in my life than I realized, but I also understood that what others meant for bad, God meant for my good, as it was He who has sustained me mentally, physically, emotionally, and spiritually thus far. I tell myself a lot that it is only because of God's grace that I am still alive and have my sanity when I should be insane, walking the streets talking to myself or in a psychiatric ward. I also concluded that God knew when He formed me in my mother's womb what I would and would not be able to withstand in this world when I came out, and therefore was preparing me even before I knew it.

Chapter 2

Silent Wail

"Remember your word to your servant, for you have given me hope. My comfort in my suffering is this: Your promise preserves my life." **Psalms 119:49-50**

During my childhood and teenage years, I was pretty much a tomboy. I wasn't "girlie" at all and although my mother put me in dresses and dolled up my hair, I would still go outside to play touch football or run relay races with the boys. I really enjoyed hanging out with my male cousins. They were overprotective of me and let me hang around because I wasn't bratty, and also because my dad had bought me an air hockey table, which they thought was cool.

When my mother migrated from Mississippi to Chicago to be with her siblings while my father was in the Army, my Aunt Dorothy (whom I affectionately call Momtie) and Uncle Jack helped my mother raise me. This created an amazing bond between us and their two sons. I considered the oldest, Marcus, the big brother I never had and the youngest, Marlon, my little brother. I was at their house constantly; it became like my second home, and I became their surrogate daughter, as did my siblings when they came along. When you are a child or teenager, the thought of death never enters your mind, so when it does happen, how you react to it depends on how it affects you personally. I would find this out at the age of fourteen.

I had just entered my freshman year of high school, and everything was great—until it wasn't. Remember previously when I spoke about purposely blocking out certain memories? Well, this was one of them. For a long time, almost into my adult years, my anger kept me from wanting to go visit my aunt and uncle's house. The place I had considered safe, fun, and joy-filled now made me feel grief, sadness, confusion, and even hatred. I wondered how someone could be so selfish not to give a thought to how the repercussions of their actions could affect an entire family—and most importantly, me! My big brother, someone I loved, confided in, and joked around with, who taught me how to DJ and treated me like his sister as if his own mother had birthed me, committed suicide, and I was the one who found him. I remember every detail vividly like it was yesterday. At the time I don't think I really knew what trauma was, but I know I was affected greatly by his death, especially emotionally. Once I was able to allow myself to try to heal from it, I had to take small baby steps—literally, starting with going over and just sitting on the front porch. I then worked up to moving my way into the house. It took me months to go upstairs, where his room and the bathroom were located. It took years for me to go into the room that was once his, where I found him.

It wasn't until my late twenties that I realized that I was still affected emotionally by his death; my own attempted suicide made me realize how traumatized I really was. I even got angry at myself for being so thoughtless as to attempt to do something that I was still angry at him for. All I could see was his face in the mirror, which is what stopped me. I knew I needed help. At the time, I wasn't in church, but I've always had what I considered a relationship with God. I repented and prayed for forgiveness, not only for me, but for Marcus. I cried until I couldn't cry anymore. No one knew the grief that I had dealt with for all those years, not even his parents.

Besides God, I went to the one person that I knew would be able to help me as well. You see, my Aunt Dorothy is the family prayer warrior. She is strong and the one whom everyone leans on in times of distress. Her strength and faith in God are awe-inspiring and something to witness. Even in her son's death, her strength got everyone else in the family through. I wanted to glean from her and learn how I could come to be as strong in the Lord as she was. I was taught that prayer and worship were the two key components in addition to trusting God to do the rest. As I began to heal, it still took me years and even some therapy, but I did it. This was the beginning…my journey to becoming a worshipper.

Chapter 3

Now It's Personal

"For no one is cast off by the Lord forever. Though he brings grief, he will show compassion, so great is his unfailing love. For he does not willingly bring affliction or grief to anyone." **Lamentations 3:31-33**

Little did I know that I was about to experience my journey to worship sooner rather than later, and that it would begin with an extreme amount of wailing—wailing that sounded like it would never end, due to the loss of my first child.

At nineteen, having just graduated from high school, I learned that I was pregnant. I thought I had mistakenly urinated on myself, when, in actuality, my bag of waters had ruptured. The interesting part of all this is that I

8

did NOT know that I was pregnant! I was still having a menstrual cycle and had not been in a relationship in months. Unbeknownst to me, I was going into labor. *Shock* is not the word to describe what I felt; *terrified* sums it up better. By the time I got to the emergency room, my labor had progressed and I was experiencing contractions. I learned via ultrasound that I was thirty-two weeks pregnant, there was no fetal heartbeat, and because I was in active labor, I had to deliver my deceased child, which was a boy. I could not process the information or instructions being given to me, as things were moving so quickly in the environment, my body, and my mind.

I remember the fear, confusion, and stupidity I felt. How could I not know that I was carrying a life inside of me? Guilt overtook my emotions. This was a trauma that I would endure alone; my shameful secret that I couldn't and wouldn't tell anyone, because who would believe me? I withdrew into an emotional and mental zombie. I knew God and felt I had developed a fairly good relationship with Him. I know He knew what I was going through, because He knows what's going to happen before we do, but I still couldn't understand why He had allowed this to happen to me. In fact, this would be a question I would ask six more times during my lifetime, as I've probably had every type of pregnancy loss possible. From stillbirth to ectopic pregnancy, molar pregnancy, dilation and curettage, and regular miscarriage, I have seven "angel babies" out of a total of eight pregnancies. After my third pregnancy, which was an ectopic pregnancy, I learned that I could no longer conceive naturally due to having only one fallopian tube, which was also covered in scar tissue. This meant that I would only be able to conceive via artificial insemination, *in vitro* fertilization, or God's will. In June 2003, my son, whom I affectionately call my "miracle," was born via *in vitro* fertilization from my first marriage and is the only living child I have, although he almost didn't make it. He is now nineteen years old.

In 2014 I remarried, and in 2015 I went through my last attempt at trying to conceive via *in vitro* fertilization, as it was the last one my insurance would pay for. I had gone through this three times before so I knew the pros and cons of what to expect and was also ready to accept whatever God's will was. By this time my relationship with my Lord and Savior was strong. I was able to conceive, and my husband and I were ecstatic. We were picking out names and everything. My husband doesn't have any biological children, but he has raised our son as if he were his own since he was twelve.

Then the unthinkable happened. Remember, I was willing to accept God's will, right? WRONG! This turned out to be the worst loss of them all! This was different because my belief and trust in God and His promise that this pregnancy was going to prosper was not only for me but for my husband. I was heartbroken, to say the least, and my spirit was crushed. Although my husband understood what could happen and was lovingly accepting of it, I was not, and my heart ached for him. I was not angry, but furious! It was so bad that my husband was concerned. If anything, he should have been more upset, but he wasn't. It was like I couldn't control it. I shut out everyone and everything. My fury turned into sadness and my sadness into depression.

I was attending the Eagles International Institute School of Worship Arts Pageantry course online and I dropped my class. I wanted no part of it. Transparent Moment: *After seeing your child having to pass through your body for an entire week, what kind of God would do that to you?* is what I kept asking myself. I stopped listening to the music I loved and knew would get me through during this traumatic time. I almost quit my job. Prayer? Ha! Not from these lips. My husband's concern for me grew into fear as he was trying his best to help me work through this process, but I had basically shut him out too. I was deeply depressed. In addition to him praying for me and over me, he also reached out to those in our tribe who he knew would do the same. Condemnation set in strongly. Condemnation because I knew better to be feeling this way. I knew where I was in my relationship with God, but mentally and emotionally, I didn't care. I was NOT ok, and I wanted to wallow in that feeling. People could see the difference in me physically as well. When I decided to go back to work, this office "prayer warrior" was now in a broken relationship with God. To add to my pain, I had to work with a physician who was pregnant. Who does that? This was evil and uncaring in my opinion. I didn't want to hear about anything pertaining to pregnancy nor even see or hear a commercial because I would burst into tears. Was I grateful for the miracle child God so graciously granted me? Entirely! He almost died during childbirth, and everything I do, I do for him. Nevertheless, the grief of this loss wasn't only about me; it was the pain of not being able to carry our child to term for my husband. I felt like he had been robbed and it was my fault. The guilt and shame were sometimes unimaginable and if one more person told me, "God won't put more on you than you could bear," I was going to scream! This lasted for an entire year. I barely saw or spoke to anyone outside of going to work.

In March of 2016, I was invited to a workshop being taught by my mentor, Dr. Kina Arnold, whom I now consider my big sister. Besides my husband, she was one who consistently checked on me and would not give up on me. I wasn't going to go but was encouraged by my husband to do so, as he was still deeply concerned for my wellbeing since I refused to seek professional help. I went to the class, and she was surprised to see me. She let me know that showing up was a start and I didn't have to participate in any way besides listening. To her, this was my first step and attempt at getting back into God's presence. Her workshop was entitled "Fragrance at His Altar" and she had a replica of the Altar of Incense. She spoke about how the fragrance we offer up to God reflects how we see ourselves and our relationship with Him. This was a profound statement because at that time I was feeling like trash and therefore treating God like trash because that was how I felt. I experienced my first outward wail. A cry out to God to say that I was sorry, so sorry, and to ask Him to forgive me!

I could not believe that I had gotten to the point of basically cutting Him out of my life. In the midst of my sobbing, I was reminded that although I ran away from God, He never left my side. My revelation…God Waited for Me! He didn't have to, but because He loves me more than I love myself, He allowed me to go through this process and still met me where I was with open arms. Just as an earthly parent would do their own child. Oh, how He loves me in spite of me.

This began my search into getting to know more about worship and getting in the presence of God. Not only that, going through this experience would allow me the opportunity in 2018 to help my dear friend Tiffany Harvey, who is now my covenant sister, navigate through a similar journey. The difference was by then I had gained the spiritual tools to help guide her to not go down the same dark valley that I did. But if she happened to end up there, she would know that both God and I would be waiting for her with open arms until she saw the light and was able to find that peace and comfort for herself. When she crossed over from her journey, she indeed found the strength and resilience to get into Gods' presence. Because of her perseverance and obedience to worship even during some of her hardest moments, their family was blessed with a beautiful daughter Charity Grace who is a year old at the time of this writing.

Chapter 4

Sister Sister

"The Lord gives strength to his people; The Lord blesses his people with peace." **Psalms 29:11**

As previously stated, I am the oldest of my siblings and my sister Teia was the second born. It's funny when I tell this story, but at the time it wasn't because I was eight years old, selfish, and didn't want a sibling. What I was told is that when my mother was in the hospital delivering Teia, my Aunt Dorothy was in the hospital with me because I had suddenly gotten violently ill. No one could figure out what was wrong with me. It was even baffling to the doctors until one question was asked: "Is there something going on that may cause her to have some type of trauma?" My aunt answered, "Her mother is in the hospital delivering her sister." Doctor's diagnosis: "Trauma due to mother having a baby." Me: "I don't want her! Take her back where she came from!"

I was angry and so upset I made myself physically sick! Someone was moving in on my territory and threatening the good thing I had as an only child, and I was furious! Needless to say, as time went on, she eventually grew on me and became the bratty, outgoing, funny, sarcastic, and sometimes rebellious little sister I came to love; she has also become an amazing mother.

In October 2004, at 24 years old, Teia was diagnosed with lupus. It took four months for our family to get an actual diagnosis. Being the oldest and working in the medical field, I took it upon myself to become her unofficial caretaker, going to doctors' appointments, making sure she had her medications, etc. On January 17, 2004, which was my birthday, Teia went into her first coma, which was totally unexpected. So unexpected that the hospital she was admitted to was not prepared to take care of someone in her condition. Because they could not move her, they had to transition her room into a trauma center and have outside physicians come to treat her. She was eventually put on life support, from which the doctors recommended that my parents remove her, which they would not. We kept daily vigils, spoke encouraging words, and played her favorite gospel music as we knew that she could hear us. After approximately three months she came out of her coma. The doctors were baffled, but we were not, because we had faith that God would allow her to live. By this time my journey to worship had become stronger, which was surprising even to me. Teia had to learn to do everything all over again, including walking, talking, writing, eating, etc., and her perseverance made her my hero. She even had to have a hip replacement. After about a year, when Teia was completely healed, she was back to her old fun-loving self. The first thing she wanted to do was go to Six Flags Great America. She even found love, which turned into her becoming a mom once again to two boys. My sister never allowed lupus to discourage her, even when she had flare ups and could barely walk, or when butterflies appeared on her face to make her look like she had leprosy.

In January of 2008, Teia unexpectedly took ill again and went into a second coma. This time it took more of a toll on her body than her previous experience had. Although she fought like before, unfortunately, my sister did not win this fight. What I found ironic about this time was that in my heart I knew that she would not overcome, and I was at peace with that. I was at peace because my worship and the time that I spent with God had increased. Also, because I was with my sister throughout her journey, I was able to confidently say that she had fought a good fight.

So much so that when I felt she was in the stages of taking her last breaths, I whispered in her ear that it was OK and assured her that her boys would be taken care of. I knew that she understood me because one lone tear rolled down her cheek. Teia went to be with the Lord on January 7, 2008, when her youngest son was only seven months old.

The grace that God extended to me to be able to handle my sister's death was because of my worship to Him during her entire journey. I was able to be the strength for both my parents and my siblings. The death of my sister most definitely changed all our lives; my parents lost a daughter, my nephews lost a mother, and my siblings and I lost our sister. Worship kept me and I was able to boldly stand on God's word. Because of this I was able to be the comforter to others in our extended family and also to her friends, whose lives she touched deeply.

My worship allowed me to give God all the glory for allowing me to have my sister in my life for 28 years. Knowing that she impacted so many people with her smile, sense of humor, and genuine love for them made me proud to call her my sister.

Chapter 5
Suddenly

"As a mother comforts her child, so will I in turn comfort you; and you will be comforted over Jerusalem." **Isaiah 66:13 NIV**

"I'll always love my momma! She's my favorite girl! You only get one, you only get one, yeah!" My mom Idella was named after her grandmother and was affectionately known as Dell. My parents had known each other since they were children and married after my mother graduated high school. Mommy was pregnant with me when she moved from Memphis to Chicago to be with the rest of her siblings and their families, as my father was still in the Army and she was the last one to leave home. My mom was a stay-at-home mom until my youngest sibling graduated high school; that's when she decided to work as a caretaker for the elderly. As I was the firstborn, she dressed me up like a baby doll and it was mother, father, and daughter for eight years until my sibling came. We were truly blessed to have our mother home with us every day. We always came home from school to a hot meal. She combed our hair until we graduated high school and kept every item of importance from our school achievements: school pictures, progress reports, prom photos, play bills, etc., and did the same for her grandchildren as they went through school.

My mom had a beautiful smile and gorgeous thick hair that I inherited. She loved her girls, was an amazing cook, could sew anything, and was also the disciplinarian. She loved her grandchildren, spoiled them rotten, and often let them get away with things she wouldn't let us do at their age. She often had no filter when letting you know how she felt and was not emotionally expressive. It took me years into my adulthood, but eventually I got her be more expressive about her feelings verbally. We knew she loved us but wanted to hear her say it. Being the oldest, I wanted to make my parents proud, especially my mom. We had a good relationship, but I was a daddy's girl at heart. As I got into my adult years our relationship evolved, and the last time I saw her I was lying next to her like I was an only child again and telling her how much I loved her.

On October 24, 2019, I was in Dallas, TX attending the gathering of the Eagles International Training Institute Worship Summit. I was on a break from rehearsal when I noticed numerous missed calls on my phone, at which point I called my husband. He asked me where I was, who was with me, and if I was able to sit and talk. He then proceeded to tell me that my mother had passed suddenly. I was baffled and asked him what he meant. As he started speaking again that, was when I lost it. *No! No! No! No! No! No! No!* followed by a loud wail. My mentor, Dr. Kina, ran to grab the phone as I started walking towards her and I collapsed into her arms. She pulled me to the floor as she wrapped both her arms and legs around me. Through my sobs and tears I heard cries of "Lord Jesus," "Pray," "Go get so and so," and Dr. Kina speaking to my husband on the phone receiving instruction as she was also giving instruction. I think I may have even passed out for a moment because I remember wailing again and not being able to see anything through my tears. I remember confusion, on top of confusion, on top of confusion. *What, how, when, where?* was running through my mind, and then the thought of *I have to go.* But again, how? I did not understand. I had just seen my mother Tuesday prior to leaving and she was fine. Today was Thursday. Multiple prayers going forth and the speaking of heavenly languages is what I remember most in that moment, followed by the thought of my father and siblings. *What are we going to do now? Mommy is gone! How am I going to tell my son? Mommy is gone!!!*

My cousin who also stays in Texas was able to be contacted and he was able to come pick me up from the hotel to take me to the airport, but I was not able to get a flight out until

Friday morning, so I spent the night with him. This felt like the longest night of my life. I did not want to talk to anyone unless it was my father or siblings. I pushed myself to get all of my emotions out before I got on the airplane. Some people were looking at me like I was crazy, but I didn't care. During the flight and passing through the clouds, I felt a surprising calmness creeping over me because God reminded me that I was able to love on my mother before I left. That's when tears started to flow. However, these were not tears of sorrow, but of gratefulness and thanksgiving.

When my father picked me up from the airport, I saw the hurt in his face, but I also saw how he was trying to be strong for his daughters. At this time my parents had been married for 49 years, and my father had suddenly lost his life partner and childhood friend. I could not fathom the heartache that he was experiencing. What I learned was that my mother had a heart attack while waiting for my father to pick her up from her client's house where she worked as a caregiver.

When my father arrived, my mother was already deceased. How could this be? You wake up with someone and that same day you go home alone. Things moved pretty quickly when making arrangements for my mother's funeral. Because I was the oldest, I was there to assist my father in the decision making. This was a process that I was not ready for, but God gave me the grace to endure just as He had done when Teia transitioned. The strength that I was endowed with amazed even me. Prayer and worship were my portion because I knew that was going to be the only way that I would be able to stand strong for my father and siblings. I was also amazed at the strength of my father, but he was a worshipper as well and stood firm on the word of God. My siblings and I made a pact that we would surround our father with as much love as we could give him because it was just us now, and that was exactly what we did.

Chapter 6

Brokenhearted

"Praise be to the God and Father of our Lord Jesus Christ, the Father of compassion and the God of all comfort, who comforts us in all our troubles, so that we can comfort those in any trouble with the comfort we ourselves receive from God." **2 Corinthians 1:3-4**

"Hey, Number 1!" is what he would say when I called or he saw me, as I was his firstborn. A True Daddy's Girl; that's me! My father AC was the nurturer of our family, from whom I got my work ethic and my sense of humor. Whenever I needed my dad, there wasn't a time he didn't come through for me. You couldn't say anything bad about him or I was ready to fight you. My daddy was my biggest supporter, especially when it came to ministry, and even when he didn't agree with some of my life's decisions. I was considered my father's twin. Wherever he went I wanted to go. My daddy played softball, so I played softball. He bought me a drum set and an air hockey table and I played with those more than I did my dolls. It is because of my daddy that I love rollercoasters, music, and dancing. My siblings and I even played instruments, which he also did when he was in high school.

My daddy was strong willed and sometimes stubborn. He overworked himself, but also loved his family and God. After the loss of my mom, my dad put on a brave face for his girls, but we knew that deep down he was hurting, traumatized, and missing the love of his life of 49 years. My siblings and I made sure our father was okay mentally, physically, and emotionally as best as we could because we were all he had now. We all grieved in different ways during the holidays, birthdays, and anniversaries, and we survived the first year of our mother's passing together.

In March 2020, I went to Texas for a dance conference and received a call from my sister as I was on my way to the airport telling me that my father was found unconscious at home and had been rushed to the hospital. My first thought was, "Jesus! God this is *not* funny!" Here I was in Texas again but this time the call is regarding my daddy. I prayed throughout every second of the entire flight. By the time I landed my father was back at home, which I thought was too soon. It seemed strange, but I was just happy to see him. I learned that my father's blood sugar was so high it caused his blood pressure to drop and him to pass out. He was now considered a type 2 diabetic; he needed to take medication and keep track of his blood sugar levels daily. He was saddened and hurt by this new discovery regarding his health, but it made sense to me and my siblings because he had also been dealing with other health issues that he would just brush off, such as almost losing his vision. Then came COVID-19. This deadly unknown virus was now wreaking havoc on the world. No one was able to see their loved ones due to possible exposure and uncertainty about whether the virus might just cause minor illness or whether it would make you severely, even fatally, ill.

It took a toll on our family mentally and emotionally, especially because we couldn't see our father as often as we used to. We called and face timed with each other, and my father had one of my siblings and his niece staying with him, which helped to keep him company. It seemed as if our lives were standing still. As the months passed and the world was still trying to figure this virus out, our family was still trying to embrace my mother's loss, especially my father. He started giving away and donating some of her clothes and rearranging his bedroom and furniture in other parts of the house.

He was trying to figure out how to move forward without his life partner and we could see the hurt and sadness behind his eyes, especially when it came to the first anniversary of our mother's death. He also voiced thoughts about selling the childhood home my siblings grew up in.

On December 4, 2020, my sister called me to tell me that my niece found my dad unresponsive at home. I was at work and said to myself, "Here we go again!" I thought about how I was going to fuss at him like I normally do. My sister called me again and I told her I was on my way to the house, then heard the words, "Daddy's gone…" I hung up and kept driving. She called back and I didn't answer. When I got to my parents' house, I just sat in my car staring, hyperventilating, mind blank, not even sure how I had driven there. If I could have torn off the steering wheel, I would have. If my screams could have shattered the car glass, they would have.

My sister came to get me out of the car and I collapsed. She knew the insurmountable pain I was exuding. I was basically dragged to the house. This was unreal. My hero gone. Again, how? And why? This was a very cruel joke God was playing. My strength was gone. We learned after his passing that my dad had stage 3 kidney failure in addition to his diabetes and hypertension. My comprehension skills equaled zero. I couldn't function and had to take a leave of absence from work and was placed on anxiety and depression medication. I was brokenhearted and my life was shattered. The little sister now became the big sister and she, in addition to my Aunt Dorothy, had to help me with the arrangements for my father because I was barely there mentally. Then one day it dawned on me that this was also something else God was preparing me for: how to go forth to take care of family when they transition, like I did when I helped my dad with my sister and mother. Well, He could've kept this one because I didn't have the strength to do it! I was numb at my daddy's viewing and cried the entire time. I don't even remember who came to pay their respects. When it came time for the funeral I barely spoke and was a zombie.

My Aunt Dorothy had to force me to view my daddy one last time. My dad was buried with military honors and his body resides at the Abraham Lincoln Memorial Cemetery. My last goodbye was me laying my face on his United States flag-covered coffin, telling him how much I loved him and how I was going to miss him, then being honored with that same flag that is now encased and on display in the family room in our home. Now, it's just my siblings and me. Just like that, life would never be the same.

Chapter 7

Here I Am To Worship

Miriam Webster's Dictionary defines *worship* as: (v). 1. To honor or show reverence for as a divine being or supernatural power. 2. To regard with great or extravagant respect, honor, or devotion.

> (n.) 1. Reverence offered a divine being or supernatural power. 2. A form of religious practice with its creed and ritual. 3. Extravagant respect or admiration for or devotion to an object of esteem.

King James Bible defines *worship* as: 1. Excellence of character; dignity; worth; worthiness. 2. A title of honor, used in addresses to certain magistrates and other of respectable character.

Types of worship include dancing, singing, lifting of hands, bowing, clapping of hands, kneeling and praying.

"I love the Lord, for he heard my voice; he heard my cry for mercy. Because he turned his ear to me, I will call on him as long as I live." **Psalms 116:1-2**

"You, God, are my God, earnestly I seek you; I thirst for you, my whole being longs for you, in a dry and parched land where there is no water." **Psalms 63:1**

I have always been a worshipper, though I haven't always known it. Whether at home, school, or work, I've always had a tune or song in my heart that would make me want to clap my hands, lift my hands, sing, or dance to *Abba* Father. I was basically born in the church. I was an usher and I started singing in the youth choir at the age of three, then joined the young adult choir in my teens, and finally transitioned to the adult choir in my thirties. When you're a child and you see your parents take communion, the only thing you think about is wanting to get "dipped in the water" so you can finally partake of the "juice and crackers," not really understanding the true meaning of the symbolism.

It wasn't until my thirties that I realized that I didn't really grasp a true understanding of the meaning of "the body and the blood"; once I did, I rededicated my life to Christ and got baptized again. I felt a new sense of redemption after rising from the water. I felt like a new creature in Jesus and worshipped as my spirit felt free. After that, when I sang, I truly believed and had a better understanding of the words that I was saying. God was worthy of my song like never before.

With this newfound sense of worship that was growing inside of me, I began to feel constricted and yearned for more of God and His word as well. I felt that I was outgrowing the church that I had been a part of for the majority of my life and God confirmed that it was time for me to elevate my growth in Him. With that change came my transition into true authentic freedom in worship. In 2012, I found my new church home. The pastor was someone who had seen me grow up into the young woman I had become. He was a phenomenal pastor and was always obedient to the Holy Spirit. He was also a worshipper! God had guided me to right where I not only wanted but needed to be: New Christian Fellowship Missionary Baptist Church, under the leadership of Pastor Orlando Dallas.

This is where I learned to "Trust God with the consequences of my obedience." My pastor was a walking, talking, living, breathing example of worship and taught us to be the same, both biblically and through activation. Sometimes the Holy Spirit would fall on us all and would be so thick in the sanctuary that the message could not go forth and we would just worship in song with hands lifted: some on our knees, some on our faces, but everyone as one body crying out to Jesus and not wanting anything but His presence. When Pastor was diagnosed with stage 4 cancer in March 2011, he still came to service and preached as if he had never had a diagnosis. He worshipped even when he was in pain and could barely lift his hands. To witness him do this made everything I thought I understood about worship go out the window. *This* was the type of worship that I wanted to give to God. Being able to worship when you are in the lowest part of the valley, when you are not sure if you are going to make it out; yet you still give God everything that you have within you. Therefore, I watched and studied Pastor as he also encouraged and loved on his sons and daughters in the church during his own time of healing. Pastor would also have me minister in dance in addition to singing in the choir.

I believe this is where worship was truly ignited within me as I learned to yield my body as an Altar unto the Lord. Pastor would always tell me, "Get ready to be used mightily by the Master, my friend," but I really didn't understand that until many years later. Sadly, Pastor Dallas passed away in May of 2014. Before he died, I was able to visit and worship with him one more time. Yes, Pastor worshipped his way into heaven! I credit and thank him for introducing me to a true lifestyle of authentic and unapologetic worship.

The peace that I feel now when it's just me and God makes me feel as if He is focusing on me only, but I can be transparent and also say that during some of my most traumatizing moments, worship was *not* in the forefront of my mind when trying to recover from what happened to me. I had to learn through each individual journey that for me to get to into the Holy of Holies (God's Presence) I had to surrender and be open to receiving deliverance. Learning to put your emotions aside and yielding to God to allow Him to guide you through your process takes trust. Depending upon how hurt you are, that trust can fly out the window and anger, sadness, hopelessness, depression, confusion, and even defiance can develop instead. I yearned to feel the presence of God but there were times that I felt He deserted me when I needed Him the most. Even during some of my most intimate times of worship I felt alone. You cry out, but you feel no one is listening.

I've experienced rape, molestation, domestic violence, attempted suicide, and divorce, but dealing with the loss of my loved ones is what forced me to reevaluate my relationship with God. I realized that to get through my wailing process I had no other choice but to worship Him in order to survive and keep my sanity. Was it easy? Definitely Not! I even had moments of self-condemnation that were so bad that I thought God would never forgive me. Why? Because I knew better. Although I knew that God is Sovereign and He knew what was going to happen to me before I did, I still could not bring myself to get into His presence because of my hurt. Knowing that I was hurting Him was hurting me even more.

The word of God says, *"Trust in God with all your heart and lean not on your own understanding; in all your ways submit to him, and he will make your paths straight"* (**Proverbs**

3:5-6). I had to imprint this scripture in the forefront of my brain, especially when my daddy passed, because I felt that life itself was over. Besides Jesus, my daddy was my Everything! It was because of his death that I received my biggest breakthrough to becoming the worshipper that I am today. My views on worship changed, my lifestyle pertaining to worship changed, and my time spent with the Father in worship changed. I realized that there are different stages of worship that one can go through, depending on circumstances and life experiences. This form of worship that I welcomed was life changing!

Chapter 8
Worship in the Dance

"You turned my wailing into dancing; you removed my sackcloth and clothed me with joy, that my heart may sing your praise and not be silent. Lord my God I will praise you forever." **Psalms 30:11-12**

"I will build you up again, and you, Virgin Israel, will be rebuilt. Again you will take up your timbrels and go out to dance with the joyful." **Jeremiah 31:4**

"Therefore I urge you, brothers and sisters in view of God's mercy, to offer your bodies as a living sacrifice, holy and pleasing to God—this is your true and proper worship." **Romans 12:1**

When I was in my thirties I was introduced to liturgical dancing, or what the world calls "praise dancing." Prior to this my main form of worship was singing, being a conduit for the songs of God, but when I was taught how my body could be used to be the sight of God I knew that was how I wanted to give my ultimate example to Him.

As I previously stated, I've always danced. When I was in high school I got the opportunity to learn ballet, modern, jazz, African, and tap. In 2005 I became a minister of movement; a liturgical dancer. I had found something that made me feel closer to God than ever before. I loved singing, but this was different. I was now able to use my body in movement as an instrument of praise and worship. Eventually, I stopped singing in the choir and focused on dancing, which became my passion. Dancing gives me a natural high and the closeness I feel to Jesus is sometimes unexplainable. I would soon learn that it would be this form of worship that would become my source of healing from every type of trauma and loss that I've experienced.

In 2004 I went to a concert that changed my life. Little did I know that this would be my introduction into liturgical dance. What I witnessed was something I had never heard of or seen. The singing, what I now know as pageantry, the audience participation, the speaking in heavenly languages, the garments, and lastly, the dancing. Oh, my—the dancing! I never knew anything like this existed. I was mesmerized. I was at the Shekinah Glory Live video and CD recording at Valley Kingdom Ministries International Church. Then it happened: One of the psalmists, Pastor Rose Harper, asked for one of the dancers from the Unquenchable dance ministry to come on stage. After she whispered something in her ear, she took off and danced as if it was her last time on earth! I was in awe watching as she ministered under the unction of the Holy Spirit. After the service was over, I knew without a doubt in my mind that I wanted to dance for Jesus. Later in life, I would come to know this general and powerhouse in the dance who would become one of my first teachers to equip me on the biblical aspects of dance.

The Eagles Network-TEN Worldwide is founded by Apostle Dr. Pamela Hardy and its purpose is to train, equip, and educate those called to the ministries of dance, mime, pageantry, flag, drama, and worship by going through a 5-module, bi-monthly training program taught by graduates of The Eagles International Institute-EITI, also founded by Apostle Dr. Pamela Hardy. TEN also provides training for Dance Ministry leaders. I became a part of TEN Illinois Southwest in October 2013 and the first day I walked into class I thought I was going to pass out. There she was! Min. Michelle Davis, whom I had seen nine years ago, was one of the site leaders, and she was going to be one of my teachers.

I was ecstatic! I was eager to learn the biblical aspects of dance and soon learned that a lot of what I thought I was doing right was very wrong, from selecting music to choosing garments. I found that I did not understand the biblical aspects of dance at all, including the actual movements, the meaning of colors, or the importance of scriptural reference pertaining to musical selection. I was about to get a 5-module course on how to become a liturgical dancer in the biblical sense. What I was also about to learn was how to become closer to God and get into His presence, not only through the dance but by learning how to build my personal altar through worship. All of my teachers were incredible, and I developed loving and amazing relationships that I still have to this day. I went through two years of TEN for dance in 2013 and 2014, and in 2020 I became a licensed Minister of Dance after I went through a one-year, intensive, in-depth training course through EITI under the tutelage of its founder Apostle Dr. Pamela Hardy. This course trains and educates those called to the ministry, then releases them to be effective servants, teachers, and leaders who will establish the Kingdom of God in all the earth. To now be able to not only dance before the Lord as another form of worship but to be equipped to teach others how to do so as well is a blessing.

Movement has always been a part of me and is now my greatest form of worship to God. To dance before the Lord is a gift, an honor, and a privilege. When you dance, you have to be humble and have the heart of Christ. You are in worship unto the Lord as you receive from Him what He wants you to minister to His people through movement. When it came to ministry through dance, my father was my biggest supporter. It warmed my heart to look over and see his face at my graduations and other dance ministry events. Sometimes I didn't even know he was coming. His presence showed me how much he honestly loved and supported me and wanted to experience being in the presence of God himself during these times. On March 14, 2021, at a dance ministry rehearsal, I was ushered in to minister a solo to the song "What A Love" by Shekinah Glory Ministry. We were there rehearsing for their 20th year celebration of the song "Praise Is What I Do" with some of the original members of SGM. When I began to minister in movement I was ministering unto God and thinking about how much He loves me and how I love Him.

I thought about how much I wanted to pour my worship out to Him in movement, as I had been going to my classes and learning how to really get into God's presence more than ever before. It's as if it was just Jesus and me in the room by ourselves. Like the song says, "What a love, oh, oh, oh, oh." During this time, I was also still grieving from the loss of my daddy who had passed just three months prior in December 2020. Suddenly it seemed as if my grief consumed me in addition to my worship and this scream came out of nowhere. Next thing I knew I was on the ground sobbing uncontrollably and speaking in tongues. This was it! This was the position at which God was waiting patiently for me to arrive: the posture of being on my knees, my face to the ground.

Finally acknowledging and surrendering all of my hurt, pain, anger, sorrow, traumas, and depression and giving them to Him so I could receive wholeness, joy, peace, and comfort:

This was my pure and unapologetic worship to Him in spirit and truth that just so happened to be in public. God was reminding me that it is He who will carry me through this process as long as I continue to yield, worship, and seek Him. As others prayed for my deliverance and breakthrough, I thanked God and worshipped. God turned it around for me right there. No longer was I in the valley; I was rising up to walk as my mourning turned into dancing.

Chapter 9

The Worshipper In Me

"Yet a time is coming and has now come when the true worshippers will worship the Father in the Spirit and in truth, for they are the kind of worshippers the Father seeks. God is spirit, and his worshippers must worship in the Spirit and in truth." **John 4 23-24**

"Lord, our Lord, how majestic is your name in all the earth!" **Psalms 8:1**

In October 2019 I asked my covenant and Eagle sister Tammy Chambers if she would teach a class on worship for TEN in February of 2020. After praying and thinking about it, she agreed. I was happy because I knew that this would be a class that would benefit a lot of people, and I would be teaching pageantry, so to have her teaching as well was an addition to our site. What I didn't know was that this teacher would become a student.

When my father passed away, I was in the wilderness; the valley; the desert. God's presence was far from me. I withdrew from teaching pageantry because I could not focus mentally or emotionally and I felt I could not give my students the best of me. Thankfully, those students were not deprived of their learning, as my other covenant sister, Dr. Kina Arnold, stepped in to teach in my place. I was not okay! What I did not know (but God knew) was that I was going to need to take the worship class myself in order to get back into His presence.

When the class began, I welcomed it with an open heart and mind, and by the time the class was over I was worshipping with tears streaming down my face, hands lifted, and words of exaltation coming from my lips. I learned a newfound meaning of the word *Worship*. I learned that in order to worship God, I had to not only have a relationship with Him, but I had to know Him: His characteristics, attributes, nature, His many names, and that He is to be worshipped in spirit and truth. Did I mention that this was the first class, I had four modules to go, and it was virtual because the nation was still dealing with COVID-19? During these six months, I was encouraged to keep a worship journal, which I still use today to write down my thoughts, prayers, and psalms to God. It was because of this class that I learned that I needed to worship because my life truly depends on it.

On March 2, 2021, my covenant sister Tammy began to teach another class in addition to Worship called Creating with Elohim for EITI, which was a six-week course. God truly knew how much I needed Him because I was the only student in this class, and therefore our time spent as teacher and student was extremely personal. We could take our time and just talk about and love on the Creator of All Things. In this class I learned to explore, observe, and understand the significance of God's beauty in everything he has made. I learned that I am a masterpiece because I am a piece of the master and was uniquely made to give Him glory. At this point I was taking two classes that allowed me to rededicate myself to my *Abba* Father. I was reminded how loving, kind, understanding, and faithful God is because He allowed me to go through this journey just so that I could increase my relationship with Him and desire to be in His presence. Oh, what love Jesus has for me that He never left me but waited patiently and never turned His face from me. That's true love.

I've come to realize that Worship is a lifestyle. Just like you breathe air, there should be an exaltation or exhortation, whether done verbally or in your spirit, to magnify the One who created you. You may not have everything you want or need at this time, but if you are reading this book you OWE God at the very least a "Thank You, Jesus!" because you are alive and have eyes to see the words that have been written. If worship has been missing from your life, I urge you to seek more of Him daily. You don't have to go to classes like I did, but what you can do is build an Altar before Him. Build an Altar within yourself by surrendering and allowing God to breathe His Holy Spirit into you. With a yielded heart, prayer, and a receptive spirit ask God to consume you in your entirety and I promise your life will never be the same. Every day that I wake up I thank God for new mercy, ask Him to make me better than the day before, and pray to let His will be done, saying, "Here I Am Lord, Do with me what You will and to never leave my presence, for I know the only way that I will survive on this earth is with You." My existence now requires me to go immediately to God and seek His face as if my life depends on it— because it does.

My prayer is that by my sharing my journey of developing a lifestyle of worship, you will see how allowing God to be the center of your life can get you through moments of trauma and tragedy and turn them into testimonies of triumph. As I previously stated, each one of my losses yielded a different level of worship, but I continued to press until I got it deep within my mind, spirit, and soul that lifting the Name of Jesus was my only way through and would make me rise to this point of worship. Take the advice that I was given: "Trust God with the consequences of your obedience." Worship is obedience as well as sacrifice. In order to sacrifice, you have to be obedient. In your hardest moments, be obedient to God.

When you feel you don't have the strength, He will give you the power. Stay in His word, which is truth. Everything you need to draw nearer to God is there. Everything you need to help you worship is there. Deliverance, understanding, forgiveness, and, most importantly, the Love of Jesus are in His word. Remember He feels everything you feel and knows what's going to happen before you do. I speak a lifestyle of worship and a developing a deeper relationship with our Lord and Savior. May you discover freedom when you allow yourself to worship and may the presence of Jesus endow you as you build your own personal altar of sacrifice before Him.

"You have searched me, Lord, and you know me. You know when I sit and when I rise; you perceive my thoughts from afar. You discern my going out and my lying down; you are familiar with all my ways. Before a word is on my tongue you, Lord, know it completely. You hem me in behind and before, and you lay your hand upon me. Such knowledge is too wonderful for me, too lofty for me to attain. Where can I go from your Spirit? Where can I flee from your presence? If I go up to the heavens, you are there; if I make my bed in the depths, you are there. If I rise on the wings of the dawn, if I settle on the far side of the sea,

even there your hand will guide me, your right hand will hold me fast. If I say, Surely the darkness will hide me and the light become night around me, even the darkness will not be dark to you; the night will shine like the day, for darkness is as light to you. For you created my inmost being; you knit me together in my mother's womb. I praise you because I am fearfully and wonderfully made; your works are wonderful, I know that full well. My frame was not hidden from you when I was made in the secret place, when I was woven together in the depths of the earth. Your eyes saw my unformed body; all the days ordained for me were written in your book before one of them came to be. How precious to me are your thoughts, God! How vast is the sum of them! Were I to count them, they would outnumber the grains of sand—when I awake, I am still with you." **Psalms 139:1-18**

Chapter 10

Hallelujah! I'm Free!!!

"The righteous cry out, and the Lord hears them; he delivers them from all of their troubles. The Lord is close to the brokenhearted and saves those who are crushed in spirit." **Psalms 34:17-18**

El Roi-The Hebrew name for God that means "the God who sees me."

"She (Hagar) gave this name to the Lord who spoke to her: 'You are the God who sees me,' for she said, 'I have now seen the One who sees me.'" **Genesis 16:13**

When I was in my worship class, I wrote my first psalm. Although I was spending time with the Lord, I was feeling very alone and distant from Him. I was still grieving the loss of my father and now that I had no parents, I felt abandoned. I expressed my honest truth on paper and by the time I finished God reminded me that He still sees me.

EL ROI

Looking in the mirror,

But I see no reflection,

Eyes wide open staring,

As I feel the pains of rejection.

Opening my mouth,

But nothing comes out,

As I long for some type of sound,

Whether it be a whisper or shout.

Tears stream down my face,

In uncontrollable waves,

As I hold myself tight,

My mind blank in a daze.

Where Are You?

Do You See Me?

Where Are You?

Do You Hear Me?

Falling to the floor,

Face in between my knees,

As the silent tears flow,

Are You listening?

Can You See Me?

Hear My Nonverbal Cries?

Can You See Me?

The Sorrow in My Eyes?

I desire to feel You,

And I need to see You,

Help me to hear You,

As I yearn to be near You.

I Am Here My Child,

I Never Went Away,

I Kept My Promise,

I Never Went Astray.

Lift up your bowed head,

And wipe away your tears,

I know every one of your problems,

And ALL of your fears.

Stretch out your hands to Me,

As I help you stand My Child,

You were NEVER alone,

I was ALWAYS by your side.

Now rest in Me as you release your burdens,

For I am here to carry your load,

As My arms surround you place your head on My chest,

And surrender unto me EVERYTHING you want to let go.

I Am Here, I Always See You,

I Am Here, I Always Hear You,

I Am Here, I'll Always Love You,

Even when you think I'm not near.

Now dry your tears as you regain strength,

For you have work to do,

And NEVER forget that **I Am EL ROI**,

There's **NOTHING** I don't know that pertains to You!

Today I am proud to say that I am finally in the state of mind and spiritual space of worship that I have been seeking. I am even a minister of movement at the Altar Church of Worship Chicago, which is church redefined under the leadership of Worship Pastor Valencia Lacy. The Altar is a safe space for the modern-day Levite to worship unrestricted without walls or expectations in a judgement-free zone. It is a gathering for all Levites to share one heart and create one sound that will produce miracles, signs, and wonders that God wants to manifest in the earth through worship. You can even bring a pillow and blanket with you to lie out before the Lord as prayer, praise, and worship goes forth. How befitting it is that I am a part of a church where nothing but worship unto the Lord occurs.

Ministering in dance at the Altar, I was under the leadership of Minister Monica Beverly. Our ministry has over one hundred ministers of movement from different churches and community ministries in all parts of Illinois and Indiana. We even have some ministers of dance that live out of state that come to minister during special services or on special occasions. I have been a part of the ministry since February of 2020 and have developed close covenant relationships with some of the dancers. A lot of us already knew each other from either TEN or EITI, or from ministering outside of the church together. Monica and I were Eagle sisters, as we both graduated from EITI.

She became not only my leader but a friend and covenant sister whom I was honored to serve. She loved on everybody and was an amazing choreographer, and her commitment to excellence and willingness to serve at any cost were to be admired. Although in leadership at the Altar, Monica wore many hats. She was involved with several other ministries and had her own baking business where she made delicious cakes, cupcakes, and other pastries which she sometimes brought to our rehearsals. I often wondered if she slept because she was always busy doing something with her family or for the Kingdom. It's funny how you only know a person for a short time but develop a relationship where you feel like you've known each other for years. I see that as a Blessing that only God can allow to occur.

Unfortunately, and very unexpectedly, in April of 2022, while I was writing this book, Monica made her transition to her heavenly home. This was an extreme shock to her family and friends and an extremely sad time for the dance community. With tears streaming down my face as I write, I can say that I am still processing the fact that I will not see her beautiful smile or hear her boisterous laugh anymore. I can also say that it has taken me staying in a place of pure worship to get through the journey of healing. Other than when I lost my father, I have never sought the face of God and His presence like I have now.

Although I am sorrowful, God has graced me with a state of peace, because those of us who loved Monica were able to come together and celebrate her in death just as we did when she was alive. It was a grand celebration. Two, in fact; a tribute to her at the Altar Church of Worship drew over one hundred ministers of dance and almost one thousand people came to celebrate her life at her homegoing service. When you have the characteristics of God, what you do on this earth and how you love people will most definitely be remembered once you leave.

It is nothing but the grace of God, His word, and my utmost desire to want to know, feel, and smell His presence that has allowed me to be emotionally and mentally at peace in my life right now—a peace that has surpassed my own understanding. I can say without a doubt that years ago, I would have been an emotional wreck, but I have found a freedom in allowing myself to surrender completely without hesitation. It has been a journey to let go of trying to understand some things that I have no control over and to admit that it's not for me to understand in the first place, but my determination to get to where I am now was worth it. Do I still have triggers? Yes. Do I still have "life happenings?" Who doesn't? Am I still human with imperfections? Of course; who isn't? But now I speak to my mountains via worship. My God is bigger than any situation that I go through and there is nothing impossible for Him, for He has given me the victory.

> *"For everyone born of God overcomes the world. This is the victory that has overcome the world, even our faith. Who is it that overcomes the world? Only the one who believes that Jesus is the Son of God."*
> **1 John 5:4-5**

References

New International Version Bible

The Intruders–I'll Always Love My Momma: Written by Gamble & Huff/McFadden & Whitehead

Shekinah Glory Ministries–Love Medley (Beyond Measure)

Marvin Sapp–Place of Worship: Written by Jason Nelson

www.ingramcontent.com/pod-product-compliance
Lightning Source LLC
Chambersburg PA
CBHW051707090426
42736CB00013B/2574